EDGE BOOKS™

BUSTING BOREDOM

WITH ART PROJECTS

BY MARY BOONE

CAPSTONE PRESS
a capstone imprint

Edge Books are published by Capstone Press,
1710 Roe Crest Drive, North Mankato, Minnesota 56003
www.mycapstone.com

Library of Congress Cataloging-in-Publication Data
Names: Boone, Mary, 1963– author.
Title: Busting boredom with art projects / by Mary Boone.
   Description: North Mankato, Minnesota : Capstone Press, [2017] | Series: Edge
   books. Boredom busters | Includes bibliographical references and index.
Identifiers: LCCN 2016031179 | ISBN 9781515747048 (library binding) | ISBN
   9781515747161 (eBook PDF)
Subjects: LCSH: Handicraft—Juvenile literature.
Classification: LCC TT160 .B755 2017 | DDC 745.59—dc23
LC record available at https://lccn.loc.gov/2016031179

Acknowledgements
Alesha Sullivan, editor; Kyle Grenz, designer; Morgan Walters, media researcher;
Katy LaVigne, production specialist; Marcy Morin and Sarah Schuette, project
producers

Photo Credits
Capstone Studio: Karon Dubke, 5, 8, 11, 13, 15, 17, 19, 21, 23, 25, 28, 29; Shutterstock:
Bruno Ismael Silva Alves, (grunge texture) design element throughout, cheesekerbs,
(tape) Cover, grmarc, (spray can) Cover, Hein Nouwens, (hammer and nails, pliers)
Cover, idoru, (paint and brush) Cover, musmellow, (bucket) Cover, Nikitina Karina,
(string spool) Cover, vectorisland, (glue gun) Cover, vladis.studio, (pencil, scissors)
Cover

Printed and bound in the USA
010027S17

Table of Contents

GET CRAFTY!

Are you tired of playing the same old games after school? No plans on Saturday? You've come to the right place! Don't throw away that empty tin can—transform it into a mini clock. Don't know what to do with an old T-shirt? Turn it into a pillow. Express your creativity with easy-to-make arts and crafts projects, and you won't have time to be bored. Whatever you do, don't just sit there. Gather supplies, and start crafting.

You will find the process of creating is both fun and rewarding. Let your personality shine through. Choose colors, patterns, and designs that speak to you. Use the material suggestions as a guideline, but don't be afraid to try something different. Let your imagination and creativity bust your boredom. Consider giving your finished products as gifts or selling some of your creations.

SAFETY FIRST

Some of these crafts will require adult supervision, while others you'll be able to tackle on your own. Before you begin any project, make sure you have all the required tools and materials, and carefully read all the way through the instructions.

GARDEN STEPPING STONES

MATERIALS

old cloth or sheet of plastic

large, plastic plant saucer

nonstick cooking spray

protective eyewear

face mask

fast-setting concrete mix or fast-setting mortar mix

bucket

wooden spoon

water

rubber gloves

embellishments, such as glass gems, sea glass, shells, or small tiles

plastic trash bag

spray bottle filled with water

cutting board

Cooler than a plastic pink flamingo, a homemade stepping stone is a great way to personalize your yard. They also make great gifts for family members who love to garden. Craft stores often sell stepping stone kits, but they can be expensive. You can make this project for much less by purchasing supplies at a hardware store. And you can use whatever decorations you want. Are you ready to get your hands dirty? Dig in!

CAUTION:

Concrete and mortar dust can be hazardous if inhaled. Once mixed, cement can cause burns if it comes into contact with your skin. When working with concrete, protect yourself with eyeglasses or safety glasses, rubber gloves, and a face mask.

1 Protect your work surface by covering it with an old cloth or sheet of plastic. Because it's messy, you may want to do this project outside.

2 The plastic plant saucer is the stone mold. Lightly coat the saucer with nonstick cooking spray.

3 Put on protective eyewear and the face mask. With an adult's help, mix concrete or mortar mix in the bucket according to the directions on the packaging. Stir in water a little at a time, according to the directions.

4 With rubber gloves on, use your hands to scoop the concrete mixture into the plant saucer mold. Use your hands or the mixing spoon to level the surface of the concrete.

TIP:

Do not wash concrete or mortar products down the sink. To clean your bucket and gloves, wipe them with damp paper towels.

5 Pick up the filled mold and gently drop it from 3 inches (7.5 centimeters) high onto a hard, flat surface, such as the sidewalk or driveway. Do this several times to level the concrete and release trapped air bubbles.

6 Once the surface of the stepping stone is leveled, you can begin to add embellishments. You can place the decorations randomly or create a pattern. Press the embellishments gently onto the surface of the stepping stone.

7 Loosely cover your completed project with a plastic trash bag. For the next two days, lift the plastic bag and lightly spray with water once per day.

8 Let the stepping stone harden for three to four days before removing it from the mold. When it is time to remove the stone from the mold, place a cutting board on top of your mold. Flip the mold over, onto the board. The mold should lift off with ease.

9 After the stepping stone is released from the mold, let it *cure* for at least a week before placing it in your yard or walking on it.

embellishment—a decorative detail or feature added to something to make it more attractive

cure—harden; for concrete to cure, it should be left to harden in a location where the temperature is between 32 degrees and 85 degrees Fahrenheit (0 degrees to 30 degrees Celsius)

CLOCK IN A CAN

MATERIALS

empty tin can, at least 4 inches (10 cm) in diameter

water

permanent marker

hammer

large nail

fine sandpaper

paper towels or soft cloths

2 buttons, 1 inch (2.5 cm) in diameter or more

low VOC glue or hot glue gun and glue sticks

newspapers

spray paint, any color you choose

small craft clock kit and batteries

Are you always late? Want to add some pizazz to your bedroom? This clock can be personalized to fit your unique style. Paint the clock your favorite color or your favorite team's colors, add the hands, and get ready to have a great time!

TIP:

Paint in a well-ventilated area. Ideally temperatures should be between 50 and 90 degrees Fahrenheit (10 to 32 degrees Celsius). Read the label on the paint to determine how long you should wait before applying a second coat. Different brands and finishes require different drying times. Wait the recommended time before moving the project from the work area.

1 Remove the can's label, and clean the can thoroughly.

2 Fill the can ¾ full with water. Freeze overnight or until solid. The ice stabilizes the can and prevents it from bending when holes are punched in it later.

3 Using the marker, mark the center of the base of the tin can. Use the hammer and nail to make a hole on this spot. The hole should be about ³/₈ inch (1 cm) in diameter.

4 After the ice melts, lightly sand the outside of the can. Wipe with a paper towel or cloth, and allow the can to dry completely.

5 With an adult's help, use low VOC glue or a hot glue gun to fasten the 2 buttons to the can. These discs will serve as feet, allowing your clock to stand without rolling. Let the glue dry.

CAUTION:

Hot glue guns are great for crafting, but they should only be used with adult supervision. Here are some important safety tips you should always follow:

• Do not touch the hot nozzle or hot glue when working with the glue gun.

• When you're not using your glue gun, unplug it.

• When you need to set down a hot glue gun, prop it on its metal rack.

• Read safety precautions provided by the glue gun manufacturer.

• If you get hot glue on your skin, hold the burned area in ice water. If there is a serious burn, contact a medical professional immediately.

6 Place the can in a well-ventilated area. Cover your work surface with newspapers, and paint the can with the spray paint. When the first coat is dry, apply a second coat of paint. Allow the can to dry completely.

7 Follow the directions on the clock kit to install within the can.

8 Insert the battery, set the time, and never be late again!

WIND BLOWN

You'll leave no doubt about which sports team or school you support when you make—and fly—your own personalized wind sock. These can be customized for any holiday or special occasion, and they look great when a light breeze sends them fluttering. These wind socks are so easy to make that you may find yourself creating a new one for each season.

GIVE THIS A TRY:
Be creative! Alternate colors, widths, and lengths if you want.

MATERIALS

can opener

empty coffee can or other large tin can

hammer

large nail

fine sandpaper

paper towels or soft cloth

hair dryer

acrylic craft paint

foam paintbrush

assorted craft paintbrushes

ribbon, 1 to 2 inches (2.5 to 5 cm) wide

scissors

hot glue gun and glue sticks

twine, 12 to 18 inches (30.5 to 45.5 cm) long

1 With adult supervision, use a can opener to remove both ends of the empty coffee can, as well as any stickers or labels.

2 Using the hammer and nail, punch two holes on opposite sides of the can, within an inch of the top of the can.

3 Lightly sand the can with the fine sandpaper. Wipe off any sanding dust.

4 Wash the can and dry thoroughly with paper towels or a cloth. Many large cans have *seams*, so use a hair dryer to dry the water that may be trapped in these seams.

5 When the can is completely dry, begin painting using acrylic craft paint in your choice of colors. When the first coat is dry, apply a second and, if needed, a third coat of paint.

6 Once the base coat is dry, you may use another color or colors of paint to add designs of your choosing, perhaps your team logo or a favorite player's jersey number.

7 Cut the ribbon into pieces 18 to 24 inches (45.5 to 61 cm) long. Be sure to cut enough pieces to fit around the coffee can.

8 With an adult's help, use the hot glue gun to attach the ribbons inside the bottom of the can. Continue attaching ribbons until they are all the way around the inside of the can.

9 Thread the piece of twine through the holes at the top of the can. Knot the twine to create a hanger.

seam—a line along which two edges come together

T-SHIRT PILLOW

MATERIALS

T-shirt

straight pins

fabric scissors

yardstick

piece of cardboard, cut into a 2- by 2-inch (5- by-5 cm) piece

pillow stuffing

Outgrowing your favorite T-shirt or jersey doesn't mean you have to get rid of it. In fact, it can become a permanent part of your bedroom when you transform it into a pillow. The best part? This project requires absolutely no sewing!

TIP:

Any size T-shirt will work, but larger ones will allow for larger pillows.

1 Lay the T-shirt flat, design side up. With an adult's help, pin the front and back of the shirt together using straight pins. Place at least two pins on each side of the shirt design.

2 Cut a square around the design, leaving as much fabric around the design as you can. Use the yardstick to help make sure the lines are straight. The straight pins should be within the square you cut out.

3 With the two pieces of fabric still pinned together, use the piece of cardboard to cut a 2- by 2-inch (5- by 5-cm) square from each corner. Throw away the small squares of fabric.

4 Cut strips approximately ¾ inch (2 cm) wide and 2 inches (5 cm) long through both layers of fabric, along all four sides.

5 Begin to knot the pieces of fringe, tying the top tab to the bottom tab. Continue knotting until there are only six pairs of tabs untied.

6 The untied tabs are the opening through which you can stuff your pillow. Use the pillow stuffing and fill the inside to your desired firmness. Be sure to get filling into the corners of the pillow.

7 Finish knotting the tabs. Fluff your pillow, and enjoy!

STAY SHARP

You'll need sharp scissors to cut fabric with ease. If you use fabric scissors to cut paper, the blades will dull faster. Keep your fabric scissors sharp by using them only for fabric.

STRING ART

String art is a trendy, low-cost way to add art to your walls. The design is up to you—your name, an initial, sports logo, or a *geometric* shape. Don't be afraid to experiment with design and color. Best of all, you don't need tons of time to create a wall hanging that looks string-tastic!

TIP:

Any size board will work, as long as your artwork fits on it and it's not too large to hang. You can use a scrap piece of wood or purchase a piece of wood from a craft store.

1 Prep the wood board by using fine sandpaper to ensure the board is smooth. Wipe away any sanding dust using paper towels or a cloth.

2 On the back of the board, use a small nail to attach the can tabs. Attach the tab 1 inch (2.5 cm) from the top edge of the board. If your board is small, one centered tab will work. Larger, heavier boards will require two tabs. Flip the board front-side up.

3 Pick a design and print it or draw it onto a sheet of paper that fits on the board. Use tape to fasten the paper pattern to the front of the board.

MATERIALS

wood board, at least ½ inch (1.5 cm) thick

fine sandpaper

paper towels or soft cloth

small nails with heads, 1 inch (2.5 cm) long or smaller

2 soft-drink can tabs

hammer

paper and pencil

tape

needle-nose pliers

embroidery floss, heavy thread, or string

scissors

TIP:

If you want to use a word as your design, large, thick letters work best. Simple shapes, such as circles, hearts, and triangles, work great. Or you can get even more creative and use the silhouette of an animal or famous building.

geometric—to do with geometry; a geometric shape is the outside edge or surface of a figure, such as a circle, a triangle, a square, or a sphere

4 With an adult's help, hammer nails into the board according to the pattern. Space nails about ½ inch (1.5 cm) apart, and hammer the nails into the wood until they are sticking out ½ inch (1.5 cm). Small nails are easier to hammer if they are held with needle-nose pliers. When you get all the way around your design, gently pull off the paper pattern.

5 Double-knot one end of the string onto any nail on the board. While holding the string tight in one hand, pull it to the other side of the design and wrap it around any nail. Pull it across the design again and wrap it around a different nail. On every few nails, wrap the string around the nail twice to help keep the design *taut*.

6 Continue to pull the string back and forth across the design, wrapping it around different nails. You can wrap the strings randomly or in a planned pattern. You may decide to use several layers of string, changing color with each layer. Just remember to keep the string tight, and gently push the layers of string down each nail.

7 Double-knot the string onto any nail to finish the design and trim the ends. If your design includes multiple letters, continue this process until you have wrapped the nails within each letter.

TIP:
Patience is the key to success with this project. Be sure to allow time to hammer the nails in straight and level.

needle-nose pliers—a long, pointy pliers used by craftspeople and jewelry designers to bend, reposition, and snip wire

taut—stretched tight

TIN CAN LANTERN

MATERIALS

empty medium to large tin can

water

permanent marker

hammer

large nail

towel

fine sandpaper (optional)

newspapers (optional)

spray paint (optional)

candle or battery-powered string lights

Who knew an empty tin can could be upcycled into something bright and beautiful? You can use this punched-tin *luminary* outdoors, and add a candle to make it glow. Or use battery-powered string lights and you can also use the luminary indoors. Get ready to light up the night with these DIY lanterns.

TIP:

You can paint the lantern to match your room or just leave it the way it is for an industrial feel.

1 Remove the can's label, and clean the can thoroughly.

2 Fill the can ¾ full with water. Freeze overnight. The ice stabilizes the can and prevents it from bending when you punch holes in it later.

3 If you want to create a pattern on your lantern, use the marker to draw the design. Cradle the frozen can in a folded towel to protect your work surface and to prevent the can from moving.

4 Using the hammer and a nail, carefully punch holes into the can.

5 When the ice is melted and the can is thoroughly dry, decide if you want to paint the can or leave as is. If you want to paint, lightly sand the outside of the can. Wipe away any dust. Place the can in a well-ventilated area. Cover your work surface with newspapers. Spray paint the can. Wait the recommended drying time before moving the project from the work area.

TIN PUNCHING

The technique of decorating tin objects by punching holes in them has a name: "Tin punching." The craft was first practiced in Europe in the 1300s. Lanterns, boxes, and plates were often decorated by punching. The technique is still used to decorate wall hangings and wooden cabinets.

6 When the can is dry, bring your lantern outside, and place a candle inside. Or if you're indoors, place battery-powered lights inside the lantern. To save the battery, remember to turn off the lights when you're not using them.

luminary—a decorative light

EAR BUD CARRIER

MATERIALS

empty mint tin, round or rectangular

paper towels or soft cloth

decorative paper

pencil

scissors

foam brush

all-in-one glue, sealer, and finish, such as Mod Podge

embellishments, such as gems, stickers, or pictures from magazines

It's a simple fact that if you toss your ear buds in your backpack or gym bag, they're going to become a big tangled mess. This project will put an end to that frustration. Create a carrier that will keep your cords under control. Best of all, you can decorate the carrier to reflect your own personal style.

TIP:

You can add a special touch by personalizing the inside too. The inside is a great place to leave a message or add your initials. Using the same technique, attach decorative paper and seal with a couple coats of Mod Podge.

1 Wash and thoroughly dry the mint tin.

2 Place the tin on the decorative paper, and trace around both the bottom and top. Carefully cut just inside this outline so that the paper is slightly smaller than the tin surfaces. Trim as needed.

3 Using a foam brush and Mod Podge or another sealer, coat the bottom of the tin. Press one of the pieces of paper onto this surface. Use your fingers to smooth the paper, making sure there are no air bubbles trapped underneath the paper. Repeat this process with the top of the tin.

4 If desired, add embellishments to the tin. Mod Podge can be used to attach the decorations onto the top or bottom of the box.

5 Brush a smooth, even coat of Mod Podge over the top and bottom of the box, being sure to cover the edges of the decorative paper.

BEYOND BASIC BOOKENDS

MATERIALS

2 wooden bases

fine sandpaper

paper towels

low VOC glue or hot glue gun and glue sticks

2 medium-size hard plastic, metal, or wood toys

newspapers

spray paint

You can keep your books, video games, and CDs organized without sacrificing style. Create a pair—or more—of these DIY bookends. They're a cool way to preserve a part of your childhood while keeping your bedroom classy. What toy will you transform? The sky's the limit, from plastic dinosaurs and action figures to fire trucks and Lego® creations. Get imaginative!

TIP:

You can use any blocks of wood sturdy enough to hold books in place. Just be sure that they are large enough to hold your toy and small enough to fit on your shelf. If you don't have scrap wood available, you can purchase two small wooden pieces from a craft store.

1 Prepare the wooden bases by using fine sandpaper to smooth the surfaces. Wipe away any dust with a paper towel.

2 Use low VOC glue or hot glue to fasten a toy to the top of each wooden base. Be sure to position the toys so they'll look great peering out from your bookcase.

3 When the glue is dry, place the bookends in a well-ventilated area. Cover your work surface with newspapers. Spray paint the bookends.

4 When your project is dry, put the bookends to work holding up your books.

WHAT ARE VOCS?

Volatile Organic Compounds (VOCs) are carbon-based chemicals that can cause health problems if they're breathed. Many products release VOCs, including carpet, paints, varnishes, fuels, and cleaning products. Many low- and no-VOC paints and adhesives are now available. Look for these products when creating your projects.

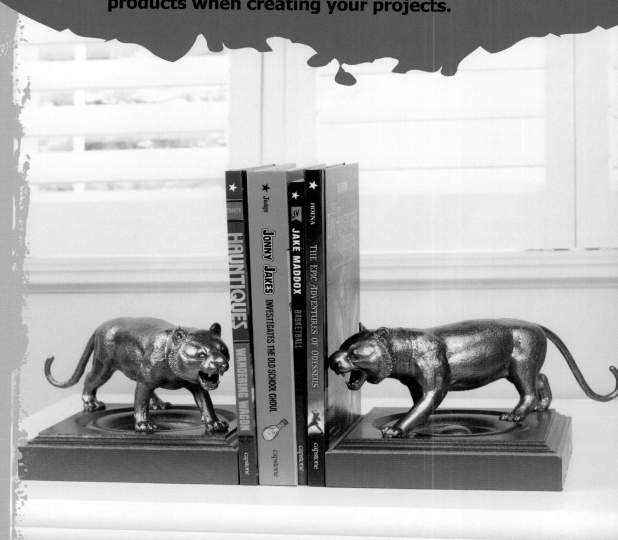

GETTING TWIGGY

MATERIALS

pruning shears

twigs

hot glue gun and glue sticks

6- to 8-inch (15- to 20.5-cm) terra-cotta pot

piece of jute twine or ribbon

scissors

potting soil and flower seeds (optional)

Plain *terra-cotta* pots are fine, but with a little time and creativity, they can be fabulous. Sure, you could paint your pot or wrap it in fabric, but with just a few twigs and small branches, you can create a "nature-ally" beautiful flowerpot.

1 Using pruning shears, trim twigs to the length of the terra-cotta pot.

2 With an adult's help, use hot glue to attach a twig to the side of the pot, from the bottom all the way to the rim. Continue to attach twigs, one at a time, very close together, until you have covered the entire flowerpot.

3 Tightly wrap twine or ribbon around the midsection of the twig-covered pot. If you're using a wide ribbon, you only want to wrap the pot one time before tying a small bow and trimming the ends. With twine or thinner ribbon, you may choose to wrap multiple times before tying and trimming.

4 You may want to fill your new flowerpot with potting soil, and plant flower seeds as directed on the packaging. Voilà!

terra-cotta—a hard, waterproof clay used in making pottery and roofs

WHAT IS TERRA-COTTA?

Terra-cotta is made from coarse, brown-red clay. It is shaped or sculpted and then fired until hard. In ancient times, it was left to harden in the hot sun or baked in the ashes of open fires. Terra-cotta pots are typically unglazed and vary in both size and cost.

SURVIVAL BRACELET

MATERIALS

2 pieces of different colored 550 parachute cord cut 5 feet (1.5 m) each

quick release buckle, ¾ inch (2 cm)

tape measure or ruler

scissors

match or lighter

pliers

Parachute cord, more commonly known as paracord, is a thin rope made of seven to nine inner strands of nylon. In an emergency, paracord can be used for shoelaces, snares, or, if you tease out the threads, as fishing lines or sewing threads. This bracelet is actually a miniature survival kit, holding 10 feet (3 m) of 550 paracord. If you needed to, you could use that cord to secure your tent, repair your backpack, or even make a splint. Are you a survivor?

1 Feed the ends of each piece of cord through the hole in the tab half of the buckle.

2 Next, feed one cord through the receptor end of the buckle, as shown in the photo. Pull the end of the buckle down the cord until the two parts of the buckle are about 8 inches (20 cm) apart. Make sure there is a loop at the end of the cord.

3 Pull the loose end of the cord through the loop to begin to form a knot around the buckle.

4 Pull the end of the cord through the loop until it's taut. There should be about 2 inches (5 cm) of cord left on the end.

5 Carefully pull the inside strands of the paracord out just a little bit, and cut the strands. Slide the colored piece of cord inside the hollowed cord.

6 With an adult's help, use the lighter to burn the frayed cord. The two cords should bond together as they heat up and melt.

7 You are about to do the cobra weave. Imagine that these cord positions are numbered 1, 2, 3, 4, with 1 at the right and 4 at the left. Begin weaving by bringing cord 4 over cords 2 and 3 and under cord 1.

8 Bring cord 1 under cords 2 and 3 and over cord 4. Pull this first knot tight.

9 That last weave started on the left, so this time you'll start on the right. Weave cord 1 under cords 2 and 3 and over cord 4. Bring cord 4 over cords 2 and 3 and under cord 1. Pull this knot tight.

10 Continue weaving, alternating from the left to the right side, until you reach the end; make sure the last portion of the weave is pulled tight against the buckle.

11 Tie one last single knot over the last portion of the weave. Pull really tight. Finishing the bracelet is a task that requires adult supervision—and it's much easier with an extra set of hands. Working with one cord at a time, pull tightly away from the bracelet. Using very sharp scissors, cut as close to the knot as you can. Be careful not to cut anything else.

12 Use the lighter or match to burn the end of the cord, where you just cut. Be careful not to melt the buckle. While the cord is still hot, use pliers to squeeze the knot together. This will flatten it and help bond the cords together.

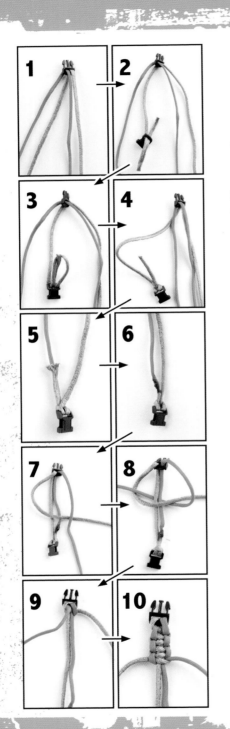

GLOSSARY

cure (KYUR)—harden; for concrete to cure, it should be left to harden in a location where the temperature is between 32 degrees and 85 degrees Fahrenheit (0 degrees to 30 degrees Celsius)

embellishment (em-BELL-ish-muhnt)—a decorative detail or feature added to something to make it more attractive

geometric (jee-uh-MET-rik)—to do with geometry; a geometric shape is the outside edge or surface of a figure, such as a circle, a triangle, a square, or a sphere

luminary (LOO-min-air-ee)—a decorative light

needle-nose pliers (NEE-duhl-nohz PLYE-urz)—a long, pointy pliers used by craftspeople and jewelry designers to bend, reposition, and snip wire

seam (SEEM)—a line along which two edges come together

taut (TAWT)—stretched tight

terra-cotta (TER-uh-KOT-uh)—a hard, waterproof clay used in making pottery and roofs

READ MORE

Stocker, Blair. *Wise Craft: Turning Thrift Store Finds, Fabric Scraps, and Natural Objects into Stuff You Love.* Philadelphia: Running Press, 2014.

Temple, Kathryn. *Drawing: The Only Drawing Book You'll Ever Need to Be the Artist You've Always Wanted to Be.* Art for Kids. New York: Sterling Children's Books, 2014.

Ventura, Marne. *Awesome Paper Projects You Can Create.* Imagine It, Build It. North Mankato, Minn.: Capstone Press, 2015.

INTERNET SITES

FactHound offers a safe, fun way to find Internet sites related to this book. All of the sites on FactHound have been researched by our staff.

Here's all you do:

Visit *www.facthound.com*

Type in this code: 9781515747048

 Check out projects, games and lots more at
www.capstonekids.com

INDEX